Community Helpers

Mayors

by Erika S. Manley

Bullfrog Books

Ideas for Parents and Teachers

Bullfrog Books let children practice reading informational text at the earliest reading levels. Repetition, familiar words, and photo labels support early readers.

Before Reading

- Discuss the cover photo. What does it tell them?

- Look at the picture glossary together. Read and discuss the words.

Read the Book

- "Walk" through the book and look at the photos. Let the child ask questions. Point out the photo labels.

- Read the book to the child, or have him or her read independently.

After Reading

- Prompt the child to think more. Ask: Do you know the mayor of your city or town? What would you like your mayor to do for your city or town?

Bullfrog Books are published by Jump!
5357 Penn Avenue South
Minneapolis, MN 55419
www.jumplibrary.com

Library of Congress Cataloging-in-Publication Data

Names: Manley, Erika S.
Title: Mayors / by Erika S. Manley.
Description: Minneapolis, MN: Jump!, [2018]
Series: Community helpers | Includes index.
Identifiers: LCCN 2016051693 (print)
LCCN 2016059640 (ebook)
ISBN 9781620316740 (hardcover: alk. paper)
ISBN 9781620317273 (pbk.)
ISBN 9781624965517 (ebook)
Subjects: LCSH:
Mayors—United States—Juvenile literature.
Classification: LCC JS356 .M365 2017 (print)
LCC JS356 (ebook) | DDC 352.23/2160973—dc23
LC record available at https://lccn.loc.gov/2016051693

Editor: Jenny Fretland VanVoorst
Book Designer: Leah Sanders
Photo Researcher: Leah Sanders

Photo Credits: Barbara Ford/iStock, cover; Yamada Taro/Getty, cover; Jason Homa/Getty, 1; Pierre Desrosiers/Shutterstock, 3; Rawpixel.com/ Shutterstock, 3, 5; Elene Elisseeva/Shutterstock, 3; Kuznetsov Alexey/Shutterstock, 4; Caiaimage/ Paul Bradbury/Getty, 6-7; Blend Images/Hill Street Studios/Getty, 8; Steve Debenport/Getty, 9, 10-11, 16-17, 20-21; Klaus Vedfelt/Getty, 12; Imagesbybarbara/iStock, 13; 4x6/iStock, 13; kali9/ Getty, 14-15; Trong Nguyen/Shutterstock, 18-19; Jack Hollingsworth/Getty, 22; Roman Motizov/ Shutterstock, 23; Mark Skalny/Shutterstock, 24.

Printed in the United States of America at Corporate Graphics in North Mankato, Minnesota.

Table of Contents

City Care

Leah wants to
be a mayor.

What do they do?

Mayors help cities work better.

They help make them safe.

They help keep them clean.

Mr. Sand wanted to
be a mayor, too.
There was an election.
People voted.

He got the most votes.

Yay!

Now he is Mayor Sand.

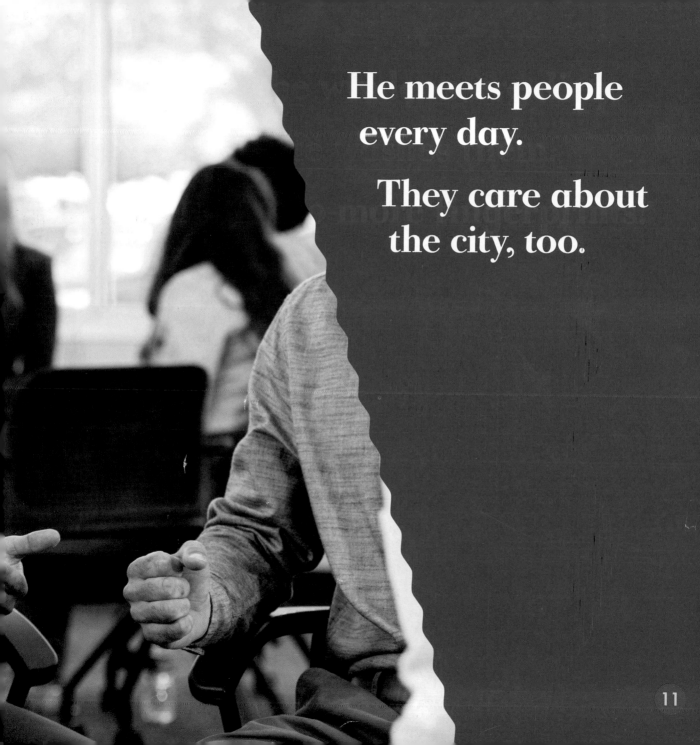

He meets people every day.

They care about the city, too.

He meets with the city council.
They make laws to help the city.

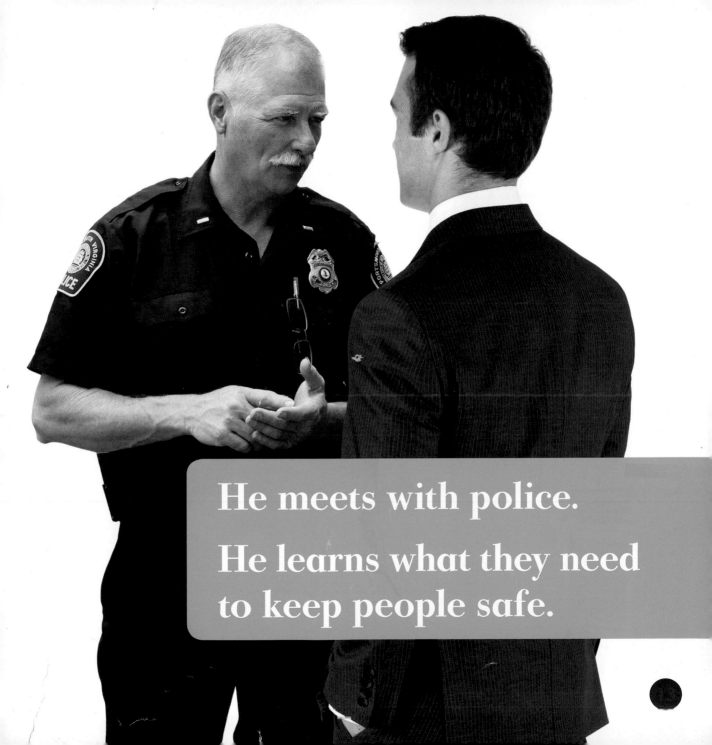

He meets with police.

He learns what they need to keep people safe.

Ms. Paz is a mayor, too.

She visits a new library.

She reads books to kids.

Fun!

ANIMALS
IN WINTER

WHAT HAPPENS IN WINTER?

Mayor Paz holds a meeting.
People come to share ideas.

What do they want?
A park.
Great idea!

Mayors do good work!

At the Mayor's Office

papers
Mayors have a lot of paperwork to deal with. They read and answer letters from citizens and review laws proposed by the city council.

suit
Mayors often wear business clothing such as a suit when meeting with people.

desk
When in their office, mayors work at a desk. It is a surface on which to review papers and use a computer. It also stores files and holds office supplies.

Picture Glossary

city council
A group of people who make and change the laws of a city.

laws
Rules that people in a community must follow.

election
A process in which people vote to choose a person for office.

voted
Formally expressed one's opinion or will, as by ballot in an election.

Index

To Learn More

Learning more is as easy as 1, 2, 3.

1) Go to www.factsurfer.com

2) Enter "mayors" into the search box.

3) Click the "Surf" button to see a list of websites.

With factsurfer.com, finding more information is just a click away.